BICYCLES

BICYCLES

ALAN DAHNSEN

An Easy-Read Fact Book
FRANKLIN WATTS I New York I London I 1978

Thanks are due to the following for permission to reproduce photographs:

Mary Evans Picture Library; Illustrated London News; Radio Times Hulton Picture Library; RAI, Amsterdam; Science Museum; Steyr-Daimler-Puch (Great Britain) Limited; Surrey County Council

Cover illustration reproduced by kind permission of Syndication International

Frontispiece: On Hammersmith Bridge, London, in the 1890's

Library of Congress Cataloging in Publication Data

Dahnsen, Alan.
  Bicycles.

  (An Easy-read fact book)
  Includes index.
  SUMMARY: Describes a variety of bicycles from the first one made in 1790 to the high-speed, multi-geared cycles of today and includes information on the basic parts of bicycles and how they work.
  1. Bicycles and tricycles—Juvenile literature.
[1. Bicycles and bicycling]   I. Title.
TL410.D34   629.22'72   78-7346
ISBN 0-531-01372-3

The first **bicycle** was made in the 1790s. It was made by a Frenchman named Monsieur de Sivrac. It was called a **célérifère** (say-lay-ri-FAIR).

As you can see, it did not have pedals. Riders used their feet to push the bicycle forward. There was no way to steer it. Riders had to go in a straight line.

Bicycles did not become popular until there were smooth roads to ride on.

Today bicycles have pedals. They are easy to steer. Many people ride them to work and to school.

This mother uses a bicycle to go shopping. Her young child sits behind her in a special seat. She puts the things she buys in the basket in front.

This French farmer uses a bicycle to go and sell onions. He can carry four big bunches of them. Two hang in front, and two in back.

Riding a bicycle is a good way to go from one place to another. You can ride four or five times as far as you can walk. You can ride much faster than you can walk.

Bicycles run without motors. They do not need fuel. They are quiet. They do not pollute the air.

Bicycles take less road space than cars. In Holland many people ride bicycles to work. That cuts down on traffic jams.

Riding a bicycle is good exercise. You use many muscles.

When you ride you have to be alert to danger. Try not to ride close to a car. Leave lots of room to stop.

Every rider must obey **safety rules**. Some basic rules are:

    1. Learn to ride in a place where there is no traffic.

    2. Learn how to start, stop, and turn safely.

    3. Be extra careful at corners and driveways.

4. Use **hand signals** when you want to turn.

5. Always ride in the same way the cars are going. Stay to the right.

6. Use the same traffic rules that car drivers use.

Many schools now give courses in safe bicycle riding.

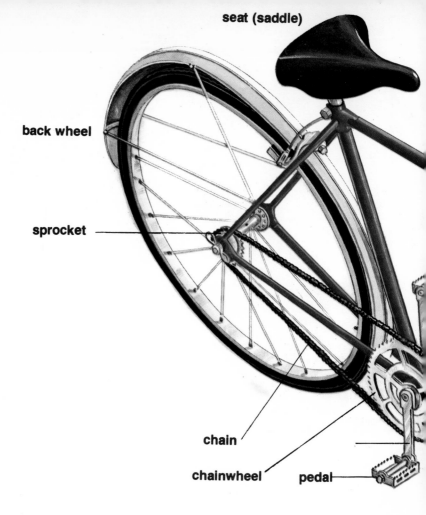

seat (saddle)

back wheel

sprocket

chain

chainwheel

pedal

Every bicycle has the same basic parts. It has a **metal frame**. It has a **saddle**, or seat. It has **handlebars** for steering. It has **brakes** for slowing down and stopping.

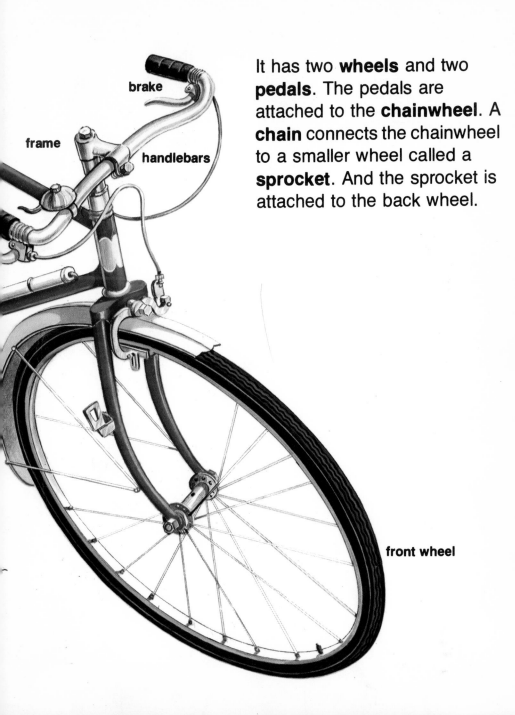

It has two **wheels** and two **pedals**. The pedals are attached to the **chainwheel**. A **chain** connects the chainwheel to a smaller wheel called a **sprocket**. And the sprocket is attached to the back wheel.

brake

frame

handlebars

front wheel

15

The chain is made of **links**. The links fit over the teeth on the chainwheel and sprocket.

When you push on the pedals the chainwheel turns. This makes the chain go round. As the chain moves, it turns the sprocket. The sprocket makes the back wheel turn.

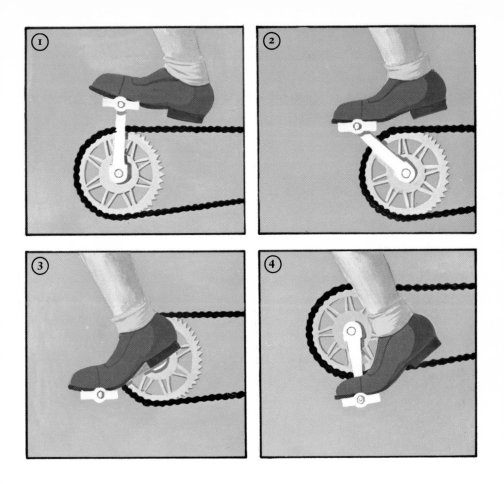

These pictures show the best way to pedal.

Use the soles of your shoes. Push the pedals with smooth, even movements. Lift your heel a little as the pedal goes down and begins to come up.

Handlebars are used to **steer** the bicycle. They help you to keep your **balance**, too.

You also must use your body to steer and balance. It helps to lean left when you make a left turn. You can go faster when you lean forward.

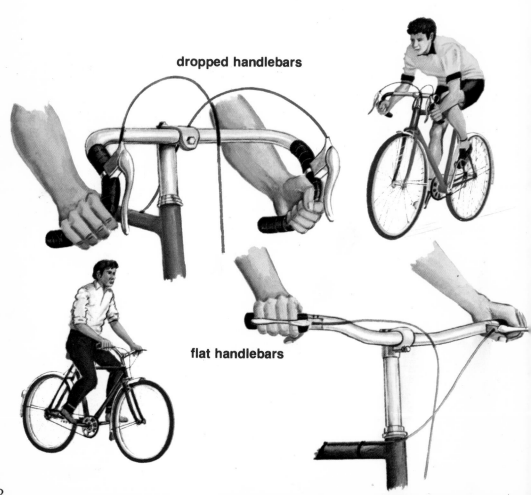

dropped handlebars

flat handlebars

Handlebars come in different shapes.

Flat handlebars are good for normal riding.

Dropped handlebars are best for riding a long way and going very fast.

High handlebars are often used on bicycles with small wheels. They look like trick bicycles, or the kind used to play bicycle polo.

high handlebars

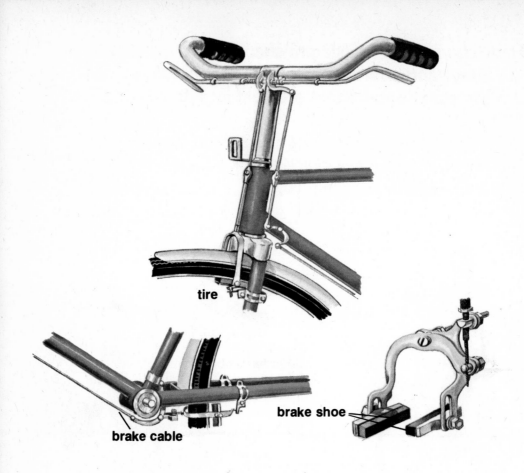

tire

brake cable

brake shoe

Brakes are an important part of a bicycle. Each brake is made up of four basic parts.

The **brake lever** is the part you press when you want to stop. There is one on each side of the handlebar. Some bicycles have foot brakes on the pedals instead.

The **brake cable** joins the lever and the brake shoe.

The **brake shoe** makes the wheel stop turning. It presses against the rim of the wheel when you press the brake lever. There is a break shoe on both the front and back wheels.

The **yoke** holds the brake shoe in place.

Press both brake levers when coming to a stop. If you use only one, that brake will wear out faster. Using one brake may also make the bicycle skid.

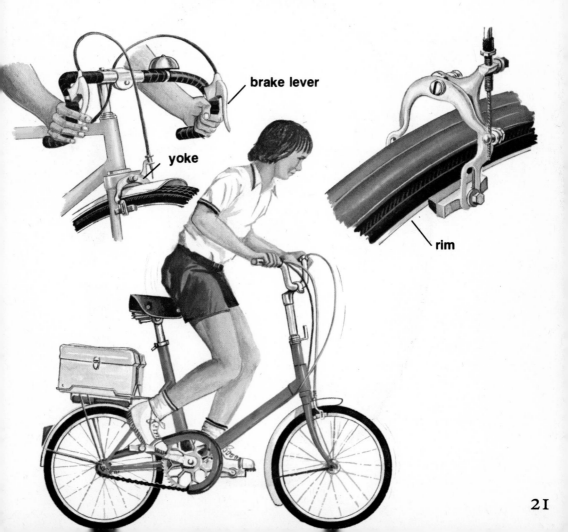

brake lever

yoke

rim

Each wheel is made up of a **tire**, a **rim**, a **hub**, an **axle**, and **spokes**. The spokes hold the rim and the hub together.

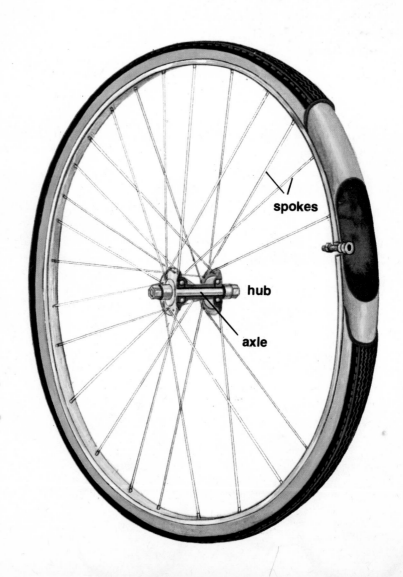

spokes

hub

axle

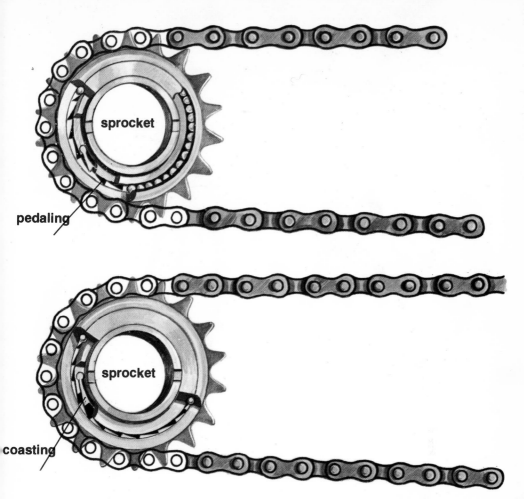

pedaling

sprocket

coasting

sprocket

The sprocket is attached to the hub of the back
wheel. When you pedal, the chain turns the sprocket.
Then the sprocket turns the wheel. When you coast,
the sprocket does not turn even though the wheel is
turning. That is because the pedals are not being
pushed.

steering head

front forks

bottom bracket

A bicycle is a simple machine. But each part must be kept in good working order for safe riding.

When any part begins to wear, it should be fixed or replaced right away.

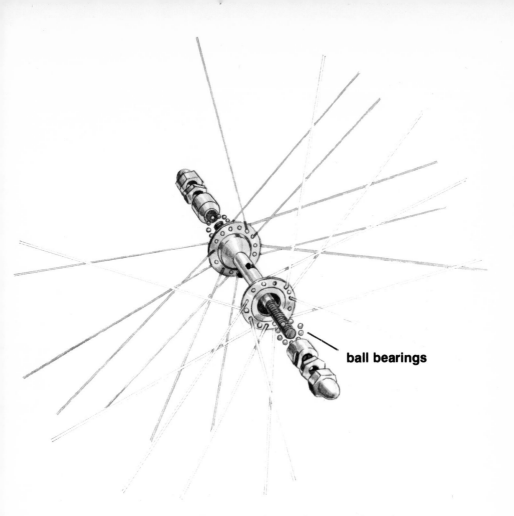

ball bearings

When you coast, the hub of the back wheel turns inside the sprocket. There are **ball bearings** between the two parts. These ball bearings help the turning parts to move smoothly.

Bicycle shops sell extras that can be added to your bicycle.

A flat **carrier** above the rear wheel is useful.

A **rear light** is a must if you ride after dark.

A **water bottle** is good to have for long rides.

carrier

rear
light

headlight

generator

When you ride at night you must have a **headlight**. A **generator** light set is the best kind to have.

Today many bicycles have three or more **gears**. They make it easier for you to pedal.

When you are starting, or riding uphill, use a low gear. You will go slowly. But you will not have to use as much effort to move ahead as you would without gears.

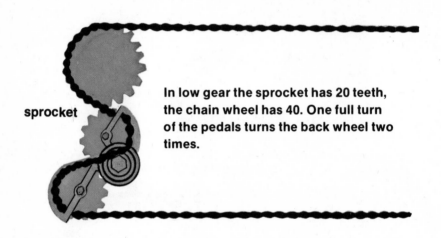

sprocket

In low gear the sprocket has 20 teeth, the chain wheel has 40. One full turn of the pedals turns the back wheel two times.

When you are moving fast on a flat road use a middle gear.

sprocket

In high gear the sprocket has 10 teeth, the chain wheel has 40. One full turn of the pedals turns the back wheel four times.

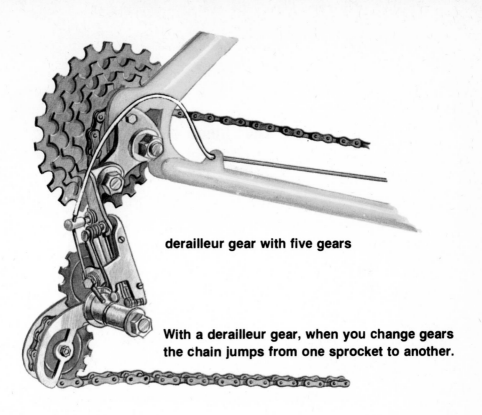

derailleur gear with five gears

With a derailleur gear, when you change gears the chain jumps from one sprocket to another.

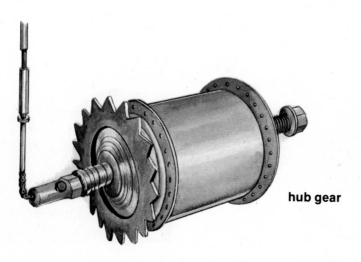

hub gear

There are two basic kinds of bicycles.

The kind with standard wheels is the most popular.

But many people like the kind with small wheels. Some small-wheeled bicycles fold up. That makes it easy to take them along on a car trip.

folding bicycle

Bicycles used for long trips or racing have standard size wheels.

small-wheeled bicycle

A bicycle must be the right size for the rider. If it is too big or too small it will be hard to ride. It will also be unsafe.

Your feet should touch the ground when you sit on the seat.

When you ride, your leg should be almost straight when the pedal is at the bottom of its turn.

The brake levers should be easy to reach.

Handlebars should be about as high as the seat. That makes you lean forward a little.

The seat should be level, or tilted up a little in front.

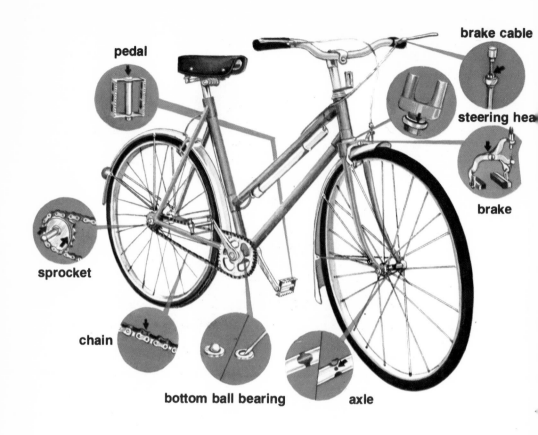

pedal

brake cable

steering hea

brake

sprocket

chain

bottom ball bearing

axle

A bicycle needs care.

The tires must have the right amount of air in them.

From time to time check all of the parts shown above. Be sure they are in good working order.

Have someone show you how to adjust the brakes. Learn how to check the chain to be sure it is not too tight or too loose.

When you are not using your bicycle, cover it. Or keep it indoors. If you leave it out, without a cover, it will rust.

These early bicycles do not look much like the ones we ride today.

In 1817 Baron Karl von Drais built the **draisienne** (draze-YEN). It was the first bicycle that could be steered.

In 1839, Kirkpatrick Macmillan made the first bicycle with pedals.

The rider pushed the pedals back and forth. This made the back wheel turn. Macmillan's bicycle never became popular.

Then in 1861 a Frenchman named Pierre Lallement made the first **velocipede** (vuh-LAH-suh-peed). It was also called the **boneshaker**.

It had heavy wheels. The pedals were attached to the front wheel. The front wheel was larger than the back wheel.

Soon lots of people were riding bicycles with big front wheels.

For a time, bicycles were made with bigger and bigger front wheels. These wheels were much less heavy than the earlier ones.

Riders could go fast. But it was hard for them to keep their balance. And it was hard to stop safely. When a rider put on the brakes, he or she might go flying over the handlebars.

People tried to make bicycles that were safer. One was called a **dicycle**. It had two wheels side by side. The rider sat between the two wheels.

There were many kinds of **tricycles**. They were very easy to ride. But because they had three wheels they were heavier than bicycles.

It was hard to turn corners with a tricycle when it was going fast.

All the early bicycles had pedals attached to the front wheels. That made it hard to move very fast. It took two pedal turns to make the wheel turn once.

Then bicycle makers thought of using chains. They made chainwheels and sprockets. They ran the chain from the chainwheel to the sprocket. They put the pedals on the chainwheel. That made bicycle riding easier and more fun.

By 1885 people were riding bicycles like the ones we ride today.

In the late 1800s and early 1900s people liked **tandem** bicycles. On these two-person bicycles one rider sat behind the other.

There were also tricycles called **sociables**. The riders sat side by side.

But times have changed. Today you never see a sociable. Now and then you may see a tandem.

INDEX

Axle, 22

Balance, 18, 40
Ball bearings, 25
Bicycle polo, 19
Bicycles
    care, 24, 34–35
    history, 5, 36–38, 40–46
    parts, 14–16, 18–23,
        25–28
    safety rules, 12–13, 26, 27
    size, 32
    types, 19, 30, 31
Boneshaker, 38
Brakes, 14, 20, 35
    cables, 20
    levers, 21
    shoes, 20

Carrier, 26
Célérifére, 5
Chain, 15, 23, 29, 35, 45
Chainwheel, 15, 16, 29, 45
Coasting, 23, 25

Derailleur gear, 29

Dicycle, 42
Draisienne, 36

Frame, 14
France, 5, 7, 38

Gears, 28, 29
Generator, 27

Handlebars, 14, 18, 19, 32
History, 5, 36–38, 40–46
Holland, 8
Hub, 22, 23, 25, 29

Lights, 26, 27
Links, 16

Pedaling, 17, 28
Pedals, 6, 15, 20, 29, 37, 38,
    45

Racing bicycles, 19, 31
Rim, 22
Rules, 10, 12–13, 26, 27

Saddle, 14, 32

Safety rules, 10, 12–13, 26, 27
Seat. *See* Saddle
Size, 32
Sociables, 46
Spokes, 22
Sprocket, 15, 16, 23, 25, 29,
    45
Steering, 5, 6, 18, 36

Tandem bicycle, 46
Teeth, 16, 29
Tires, 22, 34
Traffic rules, 13
Trick bicycle, 19
Tricycle, 43

Velocipede, 38

Water bottle, 26
Wheels, 15, 16, 20, 22, 23, 25,
    29, 30, 38, 40, 42, 43,
    45

Yoke, 21